with the Weekly Gospel

Sundays on the Go

YEAR C

ALBERT HAASE, OFM

PARACLETE PRESS
Brewster, Massachusetts

2024 First Printing

Sundays on the Go: 90 Seconds with the Weekly Gospel, Year C

ISBN 978-1-64060-924-2

Library of Congress Cataloging-in-Publication Data
Names: Haase, Albert, 1955- author.
Title: Sundays on the go, year C : 90 seconds with the weekly gospel / Albert Haase, OFM.
Description: Brewster, Massachusetts : Paraclete Press, [2024] | Summary: "Fr. Albert's words of encouragement and spiritual wisdom will help you to prepare for Sunday Eucharist and stay in touch with the Gospel all week long"-- Provided by publisher.
Identifiers: LCCN 2024004121 (print) | LCCN 2024004122 (ebook) | ISBN 9781640609242 (trade paperback) | ISBN 9781640609266 (pdf) | ISBN 9781640609259 (epub)
Subjects: LCSH: Bible. Gospels--Devotional literature. | Catholic Church--Prayers and devotions. | Common lectionary (1992). Year C. | BISAC: RELIGION / Christianity / Catholic | RELIGION / Christian Living
/ Inspirational
Classification: LCC BS2555.54 .H34 2024 (print) | LCC BS2555.54 (ebook) | DDC 252/.6--dc23/eng/20240512
LC record available at https://lccn.loc.gov/2024004121
LC ebook record available at https://lccn.loc.gov/2024004122

10 9 8 7 6 5 4 3 2 1

Published by Paraclete Press
Brewster, Massachusetts
www.paracletepress.com

Printed in the United States of America

CONTENTS

LENT

HOLY WEEK

THE EASTER SEASON

ORDINARY TIME

SOLEMNITIES AND SPECIAL FEASTS

INTRODUCTION

My first assignment as a newly ordained priest was on the pastoral staff at St. Peter's Church located in Chicago's business district commonly called "the Loop." In the early '80s, it was a hub of spiritual activity, with fourteen daily Masses and confessions from 6:30 a.m. to 7:00 p.m.

With so many daily Masses that virtually doubled on Holy Days of Obligation, the presider was always challenged to keep the homily short and to the point. Thanks to that first year of ministry, I developed the habit of preaching brief, and hopefully direct, daily homilies.

"Father Albert," Valerie recently told me, "I love catching Jesus on the run with you. Why don't you turn your pithy homilies into a book?"

Sundays on the Go: 90 Seconds with the Weekly Gospel, Years A, B, C are offered in that spirit. I have a short reflection, prayer, and reflection question for each Sunday's Gospel. I have deliberately limited myself to 170–180 words. Though occasionally offering comments on the meaning of the feast, most reflections focus on the Gospel.

In preparation for attending the Sunday Eucharist, I invite you to read the Gospel. Then read the reflection and the prayer, and conclude with the reflection question. That question can be used during the week to help you stay in touch with Sunday's Gospel.

As we journey together during Year C of the liturgical cycle, I hope we all are blessed by meeting Jesus on the go.

Albert Haase, OFM
Sunday of the Word of God

FIRST SUNDAY OF ADVENT

(LUKE 21:25–28, 34–36)

The Moment We've Been Waiting For

Today's Gospel highlights the calamitous and cataclysmic signs in the heavens, on earth, and among nations that the early Christians believed would occur when the Son of Man comes "in a cloud with power and great glory." These events will be so intense and awful that people will die of fright. But this is the very moment for which the disciples have been waiting. Because it is the moment of redemption, they should "stand erect and raise [their] heads." As contemporary disciples, we never have reason to fear the moment of Jesus's return. The Second Coming is the culmination of all history, and its hope should fuel our hearts with vigilance and fidelity.

Pray

Lord Jesus,

Our hearts can be heavy with fears and worries as we ponder the end of our lives or the world.

Grace us with joyful anticipation of that moment when salvation history is fulfilled, and you bless us with eternal life in your presence.

Amen.

Ponder

What fears do I have when I think of my own death or the end of the world?

SECOND SUNDAY OF ADVENT
(LUKE 3:1–6)

A Surprising Revelation

In today's Gospel, the evangelist is giving us more than the exact historical moment when John the Baptist emerged in the desert. He's also making a startling claim about God. Tiberius Caesar, the most powerful man in the Roman Empire, did not receive the word of God; nor did Pontius Pilate, known to be a ruthless and greedy prefect, or the tetrarchs Herod, Philip, and Lysanias. Annas and Caiaphas, the high priests who alone could enter the Holy of Holies in the Temple, did not receive the word of God. Unique among the first three Gospel writers, Luke highlights that the preaching of John was the direct result of a call from God, thus making him a prophet. God deliberately overlooked the powerful and the pious and chose a person on the periphery.

Pray

Loving God,
You choose the most unlikely of people and call them to be prophets.

Open our hearts to accept and nurture this call, if given.

Open our eyes to discover the prophets among us.

Amen.

Ponder

Who has been a surprising prophet in my life?

THIRD SUNDAY OF ADVENT
(LUKE 3:10–18)

Your Path to Holiness

Hearing John's "good news," people wanted to know how to respond. When the crowds asked, John called them to a life of charity and sharing with those who are needy. You would have expected him to tell the tax collectors, considered public sinners, to change their occupation. He didn't—he called them to do their job with fairness and integrity. Roman soldiers also wanted to respond. Rather than telling them to get discharged, John called them to stop the bullying for which they were known and to stop accepting bribes. Today's Gospel reminds us that every occupation can be a path to holiness when it is practiced with a tender heart of love and compassion.

Pray

Saint John the Baptist,

You did not require people to change their careers or lines of work to prepare for the message of Jesus.

Rather, you challenged them to live their roles and occupations with sensitive, compassionate hearts.

May we do the same.

Amen.

Ponder

How am I called to be a saint in my present role or career?

FOURTH SUNDAY OF ADVENT
(LUKE 1:39–45)

Urgent News

I couldn't wait to tell you: I'm engaged!" "I just had to pick up the phone and call. It's a boy!" Some news can't wait to be told. It needs to be blurted out. In today's Gospel, Mary traveled "in haste" to her cousin Elizabeth's home in Judah. Perhaps she wanted to share the news of her pregnancy. Perhaps she wanted to verify the truth of the angel Gabriel's words that her elderly cousin was now with child. The passage, unique in the Gospels with two pregnant women presented as the central characters, is electric with the joy and excitement of emerging new life. That new life will be announced by Elizabeth's child and incarnated in Mary's son.

Pray

Loving God,
Elizabeth and Mary played pivotal roles in the history of salvation.

The wonder and thrill of their pregnancies needed to be shared and shouted.

May all of us believe, celebrate, and proclaim "that what was spoken to [us] by the Lord would be fulfilled."

Amen.

Ponder

What recent good news was I eager to share and shout?

CHRISTMAS SEASON

THE NATIVITY OF THE LORD, VIGIL MASS

(MATTHEW 1:1–25)

The Good, the Bad, and the Ugly

Like many twenty-first-century people, the author of the Gospel of Matthew had an interest in genealogy. We can only shake our heads in disbelief as he mentions people with spotty reputations in Jesus's ancestry. There is mention of a murderer and adulterer (David), a prostitute (Rahab), a woman who pretended to be a prostitute (Tamar), a sexually forward widow (Ruth), and a woman taken in adultery (Bathsheba). Why not obliterate the memories of such people to preserve Jesus's dignity and divinity? Perhaps Matthew wanted to highlight that Jesus is truly human—one just like us—who has shady relatives with skeletons in their closets.

Pray

Jesus,

Your ancestors had flaws, weaknesses, and sins.

And yet, you not only accepted their bloodline and DNA, but you also heartily embraced them.

In doing so, you manifested the Father's unconditional love not in spite of our sin, but with our sin.

By embracing our humanity, you offer us a path to share in your divinity.

Amen.

Ponder

What relatives of mine do I hesitate to embrace because of their perceived sinfulness?

THE NATIVITY OF THE LORD
MASS AT NIGHT
(LUKE 2:1–14)

The Wonder of Weakness

Like parents remembering the arrival of each of their children, we know the details of Christmas only too well: a census, a trip to Bethlehem, a woman pregnant with her firstborn, an inn with no vacancy, a manger, swaddling clothes, shepherds keeping night watch, angels in the sky, "Glory to God in the highest and on earth peace to those on whom his favor rests." What sometimes gets lost in the details is a stunning surprise: the Lord and King of the Universe's humility, fragility, and utter dependence on two parents. This king inspires wonder by walking the way of weakness.

THE NATIVITY OF THE LORD
MASS AT NIGHT

Pray

Jesus,

You did not come to us in splendor and grandeur, riding the clouds of glory.

Perhaps you knew this might instill in us fear and dread.

Instead, you came to us as a baby who needed to be nursed, changed, and taught.

May your weakness inspire us to embrace our own fragility and dependence on your Father.

Amen.

Ponder

How does the birth of Jesus challenge me to embrace the weakness of my own humanity?

THE NATIVITY OF THE LORD,
MASS AT DAWN
(LUKE 2:15–20)

The "Thing" of Christmas

Unlike German, a very precise language with a specific word for just about anything and everything, Chinese sometimes struggles for a precise word. The common word *shìqing* ("thing"), is a case in point: it can refer to a situation, business, affair, or matter. It's used in the translation of the shepherds' statement, "Let us go, then, to Bethlehem to see this thing that has taken place, which the Lord has made known to us." The word trips, falters, and deflates before the stupendous mystery of God taking on human flesh. It subtly reminds us that the ineffable event of Christmas challenges the constraints of any human language.

THE NATIVITY OF THE LORD, MASS AT DAWN

Pray

Father,

The mystery of the Incarnation baffles us.

How can we understand or comprehend the love, creativity, and ingenuity it portrays?

As we kneel before the manger of Bethlehem, may we live with the awareness that the only adequate description of this event is the silence of wonder and awe.

Amen.

Ponder

How would I describe the meaning of Christmas to an alien from another planet?

THE NATIVITY OF THE LORD,
MASS DURING THE DAY
(JOHN 1:1–18)

The Word Became a Pilgrim

It's one of the most famous sentences from John's Gospel and an excellent description of today's feast: "And the Word became flesh and made his dwelling among us." In a culture where people brought their tents with them when traveling, the literal translation of the original Greek states the message of Christmas bluntly and concretely, ". . . and pitched his tent among us." Not only did the Eternal Word of the Father embrace our human flesh, but he also cast his lot with us and embraced the precariousness of our pilgrim way of life.

THE NATIVITY OF THE LORD,
MASS DURING THE DAY

Pray

Jesus,

By journeying to Bethlehem and pitching your tent among us, you have joined us on the pilgrimage of life.

As we experience the inconveniences of traveling with changing weather conditions, may we look to you as our guide and follow your footprints off the beaten path of this world's understanding of success and happiness.

May the journey lead us to our eternal home.

Amen.

Ponder

How has my life been a pilgrimage? Where am I headed?

THE HOLY FAMILY OF JESUS, MARY, AND JOSEPH
(LUKE 2:41–52)

A Higher Calling

Don't think that today's Gospel story, found only in Luke's Gospel, is about a precocious or disobedient twelve-year-old Jesus who slips away from his family's caravan to show off his knowledge and understanding to the teachers in Jerusalem's temple. His reply to his mother's confusion, "Did you not know that I must be in my Father's house?" betrays a self-awareness far beyond his age. That self-awareness included a higher calling given to him by his heavenly Father that superseded his family ties and cultural obligations. Like Jesus, God has given each of us a higher calling that must impact how we live and to whom we relate. May we never allow anything to distract us from it.

THE HOLY FAMILY OF JESUS, MARY, AND JOSEPH

Pray

Father of all wisdom and understanding, Your Son was aware of the mission you had given him.

Like him, may we live with the awareness and appreciation for our vocation to help make the kingdom a reality.

May nothing hinder our fidelity to it.

Amen.

Ponder

What is my higher calling and how am I being faithful to it?

SECOND SUNDAY AFTER THE NATIVITY
(JOHN 1:1–18)

Touched by God

John's Gospel begins with the very same words as the Book of Genesis, "In the beginning." In Genesis, these words are time-sensitive and note the moment of the creation of the heavens and the earth; in the Fourth Gospel, they push back even farther to the eternal existence of God. The Word was God and always abided with God. This Word, through whom "all things came to be," was the mold around which everything was created; it was like a sieve through which every created thing passed. "Without [the Word] nothing came to be." All creation—from hail to a hippopotamus to a human—has been affected by the Word made flesh. Everything has been touched by God.

Pray

Word made flesh,
Your imprint shimmers and shines in creation.

Because everything has been shaped by you, in you, and through you, every created thing becomes a ladder to you.

May we climb this ladder and be filled with wonder and awe over the myriad expressions of your divine creativity.

Amen.

Ponder

How have I been shaped by the Word?

THE EPIPHANY OF THE LORD
(MATTHEW 2:1–12)

The Gospel of the Stable's Animals

The animals in the stable at Bethlehem tell us a lot about the meaning of today's feast. There is the donkey that Mary, pregnant with Jesus, rode on. This beast of burden is not known for its intelligence. There are sheep, brought there by the shepherds. Sheep are known to be dirty and smelly. And there are the magi's three camels with the odd-looking hump on their backs. These animals proclaim their own unique gospel: if there is room in that stable, around that manger, for an unintelligent donkey, stinky sheep, and odd-looking camels, there is room in there for you and me. Jesus is the savior for all: Jew and Gentile, intelligent and ignorant, flawless and filthy, handsome and homely.

Pray

Jesus,

You did not come to us just as a redeemer for the chosen few.

You came for women and men of every race, color, gender, and religion.

May we never hesitate to kneel in your presence.

Amen.

Ponder

Why do I think I am unworthy to be in the presence of the Christ Child?

A Continuing Revelation

As he often does at important moments of Jesus's ministry, Luke presents Jesus praying after his baptism. The three Persons of the Trinity are portrayed in this prayer scene. This is surprising since the doctrine of the Trinity was not promulgated until the year 350, long after the Gospel had been written. As the community of believers meditated upon the Scriptures and the life, death, and resurrection of Jesus over hundreds of years, it gained deeper and deeper insights into the mystery of God. The mysteries of our faith are never static but continue to emerge and blossom as the Church ponders the signs, symbols, and words left to us by the four evangelists.

Pray

God,

You are an endlessly knowable personal mystery of unconditional love.

May our puny minds never box you in.

May we always be open and receptive to new insights and revelations you offer us as we meditate on the words of Sacred Scripture.

Amen.

Ponder

What have I learned about the mystery of God as I ponder Scripture?

LENT

ASH WEDNESDAY
(MATTHEW 6:1–6, 16–18)

Reboot Your Spiritual Life

Today begins the forty days of Lent. It is a sacred time of reflection and penance. It also offers us the opportunity to reboot our spiritual lives. In today's Gospel, Jesus offers us a trinity of ancient practices that not only does this but also strengthens the three important relationships in our lives. Prayer brings us in communion with God. Fasting challenges us to look at our bodies and our lifestyles and ask how we regard them. Almsgiving moves our attention away from ourselves to our neighbor. Each spiritual practice can transform a hardened heart into a fiery furnace of fidelity.

Pray

Spirit of the Living God,
Give us the grace of a prayer life that intensifies our love for you.

Help us to fast from the distractions and diversions that offer a false sense of satisfaction and security.

Break open our hearts in charitable acts of generosity.

May all our Lenten practices set us on fire with peace, love, and justice.

Amen.

Ponder

How will I practice prayer, fasting, and almsgiving during this Lenten season?

FIRST SUNDAY OF LENT
(LUKE 4:1–13)

The Word as Weapon

The devil confronts Jesus with three typical temptations with which we are all familiar: an obsession with self-preservation (turn a stone into bread), self-image (the seduction of power and glory), and self-gratification (presume heavenly support in a precarious situation). Jesus cuts the temptations off by confronting them head-on, naming them for what they are, and retorting with the truth proclaimed in Scripture. We do well to follow Jesus's example. Don't fiddle or fuss with any tempting thought, trying to justify or rationalize what it might be suggesting. Boldly stand up to any temptation with the wisdom revealed in the Word of God.

Pray

Jesus,

You were tempted in every way but never sinned.

Following your example, may we arm ourselves with a knowledge of Scripture.

In doing so, we will be able to unmask the lies and illusions the devil speaks in times of testing and temptation.

Grant us the grace to stand firm in our confrontation with evil.

Amen.

Ponder

What Scripture passages would be helpful for me to remember in times of temptation?

SECOND SUNDAY OF LENT
(LUKE 9:28B–36)

The Road to Freedom

Though Matthew, Mark, and Luke all refer to Moses's and Elijah's conversation with Jesus, only Luke specifies the subject of the conversation: the "exodus" of Jesus, a reference to the Paschal Mystery—the death, resurrection, and ascension of Jesus that will take place in Jerusalem. Luke's readers would have immediately thought of another exodus: the early Israelites' journey from Egyptian slavery to the freedom of life in the promised land. By virtue of our baptism, we too enter into the exodus of the Paschal Mystery as we journey along the spiritual life. Like the Israelites' and Jesus's, our exodus is the slow process of breaking free from the constraints and limitations of this life to enjoy the freedom of the children of God. Today's Gospel offers a glimpse of what awaits us if we remain faithful to our baptismal promises.

Pray

Jesus,
In your Transfiguration, you revealed the gift of the resurrection that awaits those who remain faithful in the journey of life.
Grant us the gift of perseverance.
Amen.

Ponder

How is my spiritual journey leading me to freedom?

THIRD SUNDAY OF LENT
(LUKE 13:1–9)

A Patient God

When Joanna hears about the continuing drought and seasonal wildfires in California, she is quick to pass judgment: "God has a way of punishing people for their sins." Jesus emphatically disagrees and urges us to keep our need for repentance and conversion foremost in our minds. He tells the parable of the fig tree that bore no fruit for three years and should be cut down. The gardener asks the orchard owner for a year to cultivate and fertilize the tree before making the final decision to cut it down. The conclusion of the parable is open-ended. We are left to decide on our own whether the fig tree responded to the loving and patient care of the gardener.

Pray

Jesus,

Like an enthusiastic gardener, you cultivated and fertilized the ground of our lives with the good news of your Father's love and compassion.

May we respond with the fruit of repentance and conversion.

May we never take for granted the patience of your Father.

Amen.

Ponder

What areas of my life still need to bear the fruit of repentance?

FOURTH SUNDAY OF LENT
(LUKE 15:1–3, 11–32)

Three Responses to Wrongdoing and Sin

We all know the arrogance and sense of entitlement that led the prodigal son to demand an early inheritance only to recklessly waste it and end up in dire straits. Are we humble enough to "come to [our] senses," recognize our mistake, and seek forgiveness? Perhaps we have been like the father whose unconditional love and deep-seated compassion do not allow for a canned apology to be recited but simply celebrates the return of someone precious to his heart. Do we reject the need to humiliate and instead shower the person with gifts? Or perhaps like the older son, we have prided ourselves on our faithful integrity and hold resentment for not being recognized. Do we shame and blame our family or swallow our pride and enter the homecoming celebration? Today's parable challenges us with three responses to wrongdoing and sin.

Pray

Jesus,
You teach us how to forgive and be forgiven.
Grant us the humility to respond appropriately.
Amen.

Ponder

When have I been like the prodigal son, the compassionate father, and the resentful older son?

FIFTH SUNDAY OF LENT
(JOHN 8:1–11)

The Blame-Shame Game

Charles is a good, practicing Catholic: he attends daily Mass, goes to confession regularly, and voluntarily abstains from eating meat on Fridays. His spiritual arrogance and religious self-righteousness make him quick to judge the spiritually weak and those who struggle with sin. In today's Gospel, Jesus famously responds to the hypocrisy of the scribes and Pharisees who seat themselves on thrones of judgment: "Let the one among you who is without sin be the first to throw a stone at her." Surprisingly, Jesus himself does not condemn the adulterous woman but encourages her to try again to live in right relationship with God and others: "Go, and from now on do not sin anymore." The blame–shame game has no place in Jesus's vision of the kingdom.

Pray

Merciful Lord,
Because of your compassionate understanding of the weakness of our human condition, you do not tolerate us pointing fingers of blame and shame at each other.

Free us from arrogant blaming and self-righteous shaming of others.

Amen.

Ponder

Who or what groups of people am I quick to judge?

HOLY WEEK

PALM SUNDAY

(LUKE 22:14–23:56)

Betrayal, Violence, and Forgiveness

Luke's passion narrative begins with a kiss—a kiss of betrayal. The betrayal escalates into violence as one of Jesus's disciples draws a sword and cuts off the right ear of the high priest's servant. Jesus commands the retaliation to stop and immediately heals the servant's ear. The betrayal continues as Peter denies Jesus three times. Jesus is ridiculed, beaten, blindfolded, treated with contempt, and mocked. He is flogged. To ensure that he dies by crucifixion and not from the beatings and exhaustion, Simon of Cyrene becomes a victim of the violence when he is forced to carry Jesus's cross. And what is Jesus's response to this betrayal, violence, and brutality? Some ancient Lucan manuscripts alone record it: "Father, forgive them, they know not what they do."

Pray

Jesus,
Amid betrayal and violence, you did not respond in kind.

Instead, you graciously absorbed it, brought it to the cross, and forgave the perpetrators.

Grant us the grace to know and use the power of forgiveness.

Amen.

Ponder

When have I offered forgiveness amid betrayal and violence?

HOLY THURSDAY
(JOHN 13:1–15)

Humility and Love

In John's description of the Last Supper, Jesus did not offer bread and wine as his body and blood to his disciples. Instead, he washed the feet of his disciples, a chore only done by the lowliest servants of the household. This act of kneeling and pouring water over the disciples' feet foreshadowed the upcoming act of humility as Jesus fell to his knees, embraced the cross, and poured out his blood. Both acts of humility were done out of love. Jesus reminded his disciples that such humble love formed the model of behavior for all who have bathed in the waters of Baptism and follow him as "teacher and master."

Pray

Loving Jesus,
The final days of your life highlighted your entire ministry of humility and love.

By emptying yourself in humility by washing feet and embracing the cross, you showed us the meaning of selfless love.

May our lives of humble love witness to our bath in the waters of Baptism.

Amen.

Ponder

In what practical ways do I live humility and love?

GOOD FRIDAY
(JOHN 18:1–19:42)

Were You There When They Crucified My Lord?

In today's Gospel, Judas accompanied the soldiers and guards who arrested Jesus. Standing around a charcoal fire, Simon Peter denied Jesus three times. Though finding no guilt in Jesus, Pilate was frightened, threatened, and pressured to punish Jesus. The crowd called for Pilate to release Barabbas and crucify Jesus. The soldiers humiliated Jesus by stripping off his clothes and dividing them into four shares. Jesus's mother and the disciple whom Jesus loved boldly stood under the cross of Jesus. Joseph of Arimathea asked for the body of Jesus to give it a proper burial. The story of Jesus's passion and death is filled with people who are fickle, fraudulent, and faithful. As twenty-first-century believers, where do we see ourselves in the story?

Pray

Jesus,

The story of your arrest, crucifixion, and death reveals the true nature of your followers' hearts.

May your valiant fidelity in embracing the cross inspire us never to shirk from the challenges of being your disciples.

Amen.

Ponder

How have I betrayed Jesus in the past week?

EASTER VIGIL
(LUKE 24:1–12)

Keep Looking for Him

I was a preschooler and fidgeting in the pews. "Mama," I asked, "what are you doing?" "I'm praying to Jesus." "Where is he?" I asked. Pointing to the tabernacle, she replied, "His special presence is in that gold box." "Why doesn't he ever come out and play with me?" I asked. "He does! You just have to keep looking for him," my mother replied. I was reminded of that advice as I pondered the words of the two men in dazzling garments: "Why do you seek the living one among the dead?" The Risen Christ is in our midst, and we find him in hallowed places: in the gathered community of believers, in the Scriptures, in the Sacrament of his body and blood. But also in the poor, the hungry, those marginalized by society and the Church, those in prison and detention centers. His presence loiters around places where life is found.

Pray

Risen Christ,
Help us to live with hearts and eyes attuned to your continuing presence.
Amen.

Ponder

When have I recognized the presence of the Risen Christ?

THE EASTER SEASON

EASTER SUNDAY, MASS DURING THE DAY

(JOHN 20:1–9)

Death is Dead

The Gospel of John is the only Gospel that tells us when Simon Peter arrived at the tomb and went in, he saw the burial cloths "and the cloth that had covered [Jesus's] head, not with the burial cloths but rolled up in a separate place." What are we to make of this curious detail about the rolled-up head covering? Scholars suggest an interesting interpretation. Unlike the resuscitated Lazarus who came out of his tomb wrapped in his burial cloths and needed to be unbound, thus suggesting he is still subject to his humanity, the Risen Christ transcended our human existence with its burial cloths. Combined with the Greek grammatical construction, the rolled-up head covering points to God's ultimate and unqualified conquest of death.

Pray

Risen Christ,

In raising you from the dead, your Father deliberately and definitively broke the bonds of death and ushered in a new and unimaginable reality.

Our Baptism offers us hope of transcending death and living in this new reality.

Amen.

Ponder

What experiences have helped me to believe that death is not the end?

SECOND SUNDAY OF EASTER
(JOHN 20:19–31)

Probe My Wounds

She sobbed over her daughter's death by suicide. "I should have seen it coming. My faith in God is destroyed." I shared with her what I have learned after five decades of reflecting on my own father's suicide. I told her that many people experience guilt for being blind to possible warning signs. I mentioned how it's difficult to believe that God judges with the quickness of a human heart—"I don't think God judges an entire life based upon a final act of desperation." And I said the wound will always remain, but it does stop bleeding. In today's Gospel, the Risen Christ still has his wounds, and in probing them, Thomas, like this woman listening to me, found the faith to call Jesus "My Lord and My God!"

Pray

Risen Christ,
Like yours, the wounds of our hearts remain—but some no longer bleed.

May we never hesitate to allow others to probe them so they might come to deeper faith in you.

Amen.

Ponder

When have others probed my wounds and rediscovered faith and hope?

THIRD SUNDAY OF EASTER
(JOHN 21:1–19)

Happiness and Holiness

Martha had been an energetic woman for most of her life. An avid tennis player and stay-at-home mother for many years, she was widowed at age forty-one and managed to single-handedly raise three of her five children still at home. Now eighty-two years old, she lives in a nursing home and spends her days in a wheelchair praying, reading, and playing cards with some residents. Asked for the secret to her happiness, she always replies, "Learn to play with the cards you are dealt. Surrender and accept whatever comes your way. Those are the secrets to my happiness." And to her holiness as well. She is a living incarnation of the old-age proverb that Jesus quotes to Peter at the conclusion of today's Gospel.

Pray

Jesus,

You offer us an example of surrender and acceptance in the final days of your earthly life.

May we live with the faith and hope that your Father never asks more of us than we can handle.

Amen.

Ponder

What do I fear and fight against in my daily life? Why?

FOURTH SUNDAY OF EASTER
(JOHN 10:27–30)

The Voice of the Good Shepherd

The Good Shepherd speaks to us, his sheep, in myriad ways. His voice is heard in the sacraments, especially the Eucharist, Reconciliation, and the Anointing of the Sick. He offers us advice through the wisdom of our elders and those family and friends who know us well. He gives encouragement to us in Scripture as well as through our favorite spiritual authors. He can be heard in the wonders of creation and in the deep silence of prayerful contemplation. He speaks to us in the situations in which we find ourselves, in our deepest feelings, and in our most creative thoughts. In every aspect of our lives, the Good Shepherd is prodding us to deeper faith in the eternal life promised in today's Gospel.

Pray

Jesus,
In the nitty-gritty of our daily lives, you speak to us.

Give us the grace to be attuned to your voice and the courage to follow you wherever you lead us.

Give us hope in your promise of eternal life.

Amen.

Ponder

Where do I hear the voice of the Good Shepherd?

FIFTH SUNDAY OF EASTER
(JOHN 13:31–33A, 34–35)

The Preeminent Sign of Discipleship

How do we show we are disciples of Jesus? By being baptized? Going to church on Sundays? The ability to pray the Lord's Prayer from memory? Incorporating prayer, fasting, and almsgiving in our lives? Important as these are, Jesus highlights the preeminent sign of discipleship in today's Gospel: "This is how all will know that you are my disciples, if you have love for one another." Jesus's life makes clear that this love is not a feeling, emotion, or sentiment. It is the radical and deliberate commitment to live a life of selfless surrender, self-denying sacrifice, and solicitous service toward others. This is the "new commandment" we are called to live in our daily lives.

Pray

Jesus,
You give us the example of perfect love as you served others, surrendered to the Father's will, and sacrificed your life.

Grant us the grace to move beyond our selfishness and live as selflessly as you.

Amen.

Ponder

In what practical ways is my Christian discipleship expressed through a loving life of surrender, sacrifice, and service toward others?

SIXTH SUNDAY OF EASTER
(JOHN 14:23–29)

A Living Sacrament

As soon as she walked into the room, I immediately knew I was in the presence of a holy person. She radiated the presence of God." Jill was describing her experience of meeting the future canonized saint, Mother Teresa of Calcutta, in Saint Louis. The saint loved Jesus so much that she readily kept his word and lived it as radically as she could in her daily life. As a result, she became a dwelling place—a living sacrament—of the divine presence as Jesus promised. Today's Gospel reminds us of an important lesson in the spiritual life: we show our love for Jesus by keeping his word—and when we do, we become receptacles and manifestations of God's presence in the world.

Pray

Jesus,

You and your Father promise to dwell in the lives of those of us who love and keep your word.

May we live in such a way that proclaims your divine presence among those we encounter in life.

Amen.

Ponder

What words of Jesus do I struggle to live by in my daily life?

SEVENTH SUNDAY OF EASTER
(JOHN 17:20–26)

The Father's Gift to Jesus

"You are such a gift to me," Andrew said. "What do you mean?" Sarah asked. He replied, "You seemingly came out of nowhere into my life. You've enriched me. On my good days, you are a source of joy and a smile. On my bad days, you are more of a help than a hindrance. You let me be the person I am called to be." In today's Gospel, Jesus acknowledges that his followers are his Father's gifts to him. As gifts, we are challenged to stand alongside Jesus, to enrich his life, to be a source of his joy, and to help him. As we do that, he finds the ability to fulfill his mission—and we discover anew our identity as his heavenly Father's gifts to him.

Pray

Father,
You did not want your Son to be alone in his ministry.

You blessed him with followers who encircled him.

May we always live with the awareness that we are your gifts to him.

Amen.

Ponder

How do I live my life as a gift to Jesus?

THE ASCENSION OF THE LORD
(LUKE 24:46–53)

Friend and Lord

In Luke's Gospel, Jesus's ascension occurs on the same day as his resurrection. This reminds us that the Resurrection is not a mere resuscitation but a majestic glorification. Recognizing Jesus as the Son of God and the Christ as he was taken up to heaven, the disciples "did him homage." The Greek word *proskuneo*, denoting awe, adoration, and worship, has the sense of "kneeling or prostrating as a sign of obeisance," "bowing the face to the ground." Though the disciples ate with Jesus, journeyed with him, joked with him, and learned from him, they now realize that theirs was not a cozy relationship among equals. As contemporary disciples, we too are invited into an intimate relationship where we share our lives with Jesus. We need to remember, however, that Jesus is not only our friend but also an object of adoration and reverence as the Son of God.

Pray

Risen Christ,
You are my friend, the Savior, and the Lord of all creation.
I adore you.
Amen.

Ponder

How do I adore and worship Jesus as the Son of God?

VIGIL OF PENTECOST
(JOHN 7:37–39)

Slake Our Spiritual Thirst

Today's Gospel occurs on "the last and greatest day of the feast" of Tabernacles. One of the feast's rituals was pouring a ceremonial libation of water, taken from the Pool of Siloam, onto the Temple's altar. This ritualized the prophecies of Zechariah 14:6 and Ezekiel 47:1–11, which spoke of water pouring out from the Temple, the center of the world, and giving life wherever it flowed. Jesus invites us to slake our thirst with him as a new temple who is the source of living water. The evangelist reminds us that the living water is the Spirit who will be poured over those who believe in Jesus.

Pray

Spirit of God,
You are the living water of life and the gift of the Risen, Glorified Jesus to those who believe in him.

Your presence in our lives illumines the ways we can slake the spiritual thirst of our hearts.

Grant us the wisdom to follow your lead.

Amen.

Ponder

How does the Holy Spirit help me slake my spiritual thirst?

PENTECOST
(JOHN 20:19–23)

The Breath of Life

The fourth Gospel is the only Gospel that records Jesus's gift of the Holy Spirit to his disciples. It occurs on Easter evening in the Upper Room. Jesus appears, offers peace, shows the marks of his crucifixion, and commissions the disciples. In Genesis, God blew the breath of life into Adam's nostrils, and Adam became a living being. Now the disciples' new spiritual life is birthed through the breath of the Risen Christ with the gift of the Spirit. And with that new life comes a share in Jesus's ministry of forgiving sins.

Pray

Risen Christ,
You have bestowed the gift of the Holy Spirit upon your community of believers.

Through your breath, you have shared the very life energy given to you when the Spirit conceived you in the Virgin's womb.

Your community is now the womb of new life that offers all sinners a chance to be born again.

May we always breathe deeply in your Spirit.

Amen.

Ponder

How is the gift of the Holy Spirit manifested in my life?

ORDINARY TIME

THE MOST HOLY TRINITY

(JOHN 16:12–15)

A Fountain Fullness

Today's Gospel suggests our knowledge of the Triune God—Father, Son, and Holy Spirit—is always incomplete, inadequate, and ever-evolving. Jesus tells his disciples he has much more to say, "but you cannot bear it now." The Spirit of truth will disclose and reveal all truth when the time is right. Despite our theological understanding of God over twenty-one centuries, there is always immensely more to learn about the endless, inaccessible mystery of the Trinity. Perhaps the famous Franciscan theologian, Saint Bonaventure, hit the nail on the head when he referred to the Triune God as a "fountain fullness," a self-revealing God constantly and continually erupting like a geyser in our lives through the wonders of creation and Scripture.

Pray

Triune God, Father, Son, and Holy Spirit,
You continually reveal truths of your Being to us.
Our puny minds will never fathom the depths of the mystery of your Triune nature.
May we always hunger for more knowledge of you.
Amen.

Ponder

How has my understanding of the Triune God changed over time?

THE MOST HOLY BODY AND BLOOD OF CHRIST

(LUKE 9:11B–17)

A Heavenly Banquet

Don't be disappointed that the Gospel for today's feast isn't one of the Last Supper accounts. Scholars tell us that Luke's account of today's miracle is rich in symbolism. Five loaves and two fish equal seven items, a number indicating perfection. The Greek word for "sit down" (*kataklino*, more accurately translated as "recline") is used expressly for banquets and connotes joy and abundance. The Greek word for "groups" (*klisia*) specifically means a group of banqueters, buttressing the dignity and hospitality of a feast. Jesus's formulaic action of taking the loaves and fish, looking up to heaven, blessing them, breaking them, and giving them to the disciples for distribution has strong Eucharistic overtones. Luke's version of this earthly miracle foreshadows and reflects the sumptuous heavenly banquet in which no one is turned away or left hungry, symbolized in the twelve baskets of leftovers.

Pray

Lord Jesus,
May our celebration of the Eucharist remind us of the heavenly banquet where all the hungers of our hearts will be satisfied.
Amen.

Ponder

What hungers of mine are satisfied in the Eucharist, and what hungers remain unsatisfied?

SECOND SUNDAY IN ORDINARY TIME
(JOHN 2:1–11)

Devotion to the Mother of Jesus

The first of seven "signs," the Fourth Gospel's designation for the miracles of Jesus that exhibit the glory of his divinity, occurs at a wedding feast in Cana and is unique to this Gospel. In a culture where weddings lasted several days and food and drink were expected to be amply available for the guests, the "mother of Jesus," never mentioned by name in John's Gospel, notices an impending embarrassment for the newlyweds and intercedes on their behalf with her son: "They have no wine." After a brief exchange with Jesus, the mother of Jesus tells the servants, "Do whatever he tells you." This story celebrates the intercessory power of the mother of Jesus. It also reminds us that all devotion to Mary and the saints should challenge us to a deeper commitment and fidelity to the teachings of Jesus.

Pray

Mother of Jesus,
May we never hesitate to invoke your intercession, knowing full well that you will call us to a deeper relationship with Jesus.
Amen.

Ponder

How does my devotion to the saints strengthen my Christian discipleship?

THIRD SUNDAY IN ORDINARY TIME
(LUKE 1:1–4; 4:14–21)

Continuing the Mission

The evangelist portrays Jesus as unrolling the scroll of the prophet Isaiah and specifically looking for a particular passage. His statement to those in the synagogue at the end of today's Gospel, "Today this Scripture passage is fulfilled in your hearing," suggests Jesus saw himself and his mission in that passage. That mission continues in the lives of his contemporary followers: Joseph brings "glad tidings to the poor" by keeping spare change on hand for those in need. Tom and Esther "proclaim liberty to captives" by monthly visits to a prison, while Lisa does so by having a pen-pal relationship with someone on death row. Bill helps the blind recover their sight by donating his used eyeglasses to be used by low-income people. Jane lets "the oppressed go free" by being informed of news at our southern border. Austin proclaims "a year acceptable to the Lord" by reminding those in his congregation that it's never too late to come closer to the Lord.

Pray

Jesus,
May we discover how to follow you.
Amen.

Ponder

How do I live out Jesus's mission statement?

FOURTH SUNDAY IN ORDINARY TIME
(LUKE 4:21–30)

A God Who Refuses to Be Boxed In

We easily put God in the box of our theological understanding and smugly declare what is and what is not the divine will. We pride ourselves on being "insiders" who know the truth while people of other faiths are "outsiders" in whom God shows little, if any, interest. We get upset and threaten anyone who challenges our monopoly on God. That's what happens in today's Gospel. The people in the synagogue think they really know Jesus—"Isn't this the son of Joseph?"—and are amazed at the words he speaks regarding the fulfillment of Scripture. Their ears no doubt perked up since this was certainly good news for them, the chosen people of God. Jesus challenges their smugness and upends their belief in knowing how God acts by reminding them how God blessed two non-Jews, the widow of Zarephath and Naaman the Syrian. God refuses to be boxed in.

Pray

Loving God,
May we always stand in awe of the mystery of your grace working among all people.
Amen.

Ponder

When has God challenged my religious and theological understanding?

FIFTH SUNDAY IN ORDINARY TIME
(LUKE 5:1–11)

Deep Water

While praying, Belinda realized she needed to seek counseling for a childhood trauma. Not having the gift for languages, Fr. Raymond nevertheless responded to the call for foreign missionaries. Peter, after a long night of fishing with nothing to show for his efforts, also encountered Jesus. Jesus told him, "Put out into deep water and lower your nets for a catch." Peter's response betrays his frustration and exhaustion: "Master, we have worked hard all night and have caught nothing, but at your command I will lower the nets." Amid his vulnerability and failure, Peter's obedience is blessed with a large catch of fish. When, like Belinda, Fr. Raymond, and Peter, we are humble enough to respond to

Jesus's call to deep water, we find ourselves abundantly blessed in ways we never thought imaginable.

Pray

Jesus,

You come to us in our weakness and vulnerability and challenge us to trust you.

May we respond with Peter's obedience.

Amen.

Ponder

When did God call me into the "deep water" of my life? How did I respond?

SIXTH SUNDAY IN ORDINARY TIME
(LUKE 6:17, 20–26)

Practical Consequences

A single mother of twins and working two jobs to make ends meet, Sadie incarnates the attitude of gratitude. As she rides the subway, she clings to her faith as tightly as she does her purse. Her joy is contagious as she shares the blessings God has given her with anyone who will listen. William, on the other hand, is CEO of a mid-size manufacturing company. His days are often filled with anxiety as he checks his company's production schedule as well as his investments on Wall Street. He walks with a furrowed brow and heavy, ponderous footsteps. Sadie and William are examples of the blessedness and woefulness found in today's Gospel. Luke's Sermon on the Plain reminds us that living as Christ's disciples has practical consequences: satisfaction, joy, and the reward of heaven.

Pray

Jesus,
Your Beatitudes reverse the practical economics and social realities of this world and offer great consolation in times of trial, distress, and suffering.
May we truly believe and live them.
Amen.

Ponder

What does my typical daily mood say about my faith?

SEVENTH SUNDAY IN ORDINARY TIME
(LUKE 6:27–38)

Six Greek Words

Sheng Xiao Dong was my best Chinese friend during my missionary years in mainland China. An atheist, he sometimes would ask me questions about Jesus, the Church, and the Catholic faith. One evening, as we ate some spicy crawfish in my favorite restaurant in Beijing, he asked, "How would you summarize all the teachings of Jesus in one sentence?" I pondered that question for a while and thought of today's Gospel. Love of enemies? Never respond with evil? Be charitable? The golden rule? Don't be judgmental? Always forgive? After a few minutes, I said, "For the measure with which you measure will in return be measured out to you." That translation of the six Greek words that conclude the Gospel captures both the call to selflessness and the judgment on selfishness at the heart of today's Gospel.

Pray

Lord,
You revealed a loving, forgiving, and generous God.
Thank you for reminding us that we will be repaid with the same love, forgiveness, and generosity that we show to others.
Amen.

Ponder

How would I answer Sheng Xiao Dong's question?

EIGHTH SUNDAY IN ORDINARY TIME
(LUKE 6:39–45)

Wood and Trees

The son of a carpenter, Jesus aptly uses the image of a splinter and a wooden beam to describe those of us who play God and sit in judgment of others. When we have the audacity to do that, we are like blind guides who lead and fall with other blind people into a pit. We need first to confront our own sins and moral failures. Jesus mixes metaphors and buttresses this teaching with an agrarian analogy of the incapability of thornbushes and brambles to produce figs and grapes. "For every tree is known by its own fruit." To ensure we understand his teaching, Jesus shows us the source of our judgmental attitudes and evil deeds: the human heart.

Pray

Lord Jesus,

Heal us of our blindness that is quick to judge others but slow to admit our own faults and failures.

Give us the courage to make an inventory of our hearts and rid ourselves of any traces of evil.

May we produce good fruit that feeds others in your kingdom.

Amen.

Ponder

What's in my heart?

NINTH SUNDAY IN ORDINARY TIME
(LUKE 7:1–10)

"Amazing" Faith

During the early months of the COVID pandemic, nine-year-old Ben told me his fourth-grade teacher, Mrs. Omir, had contracted the virus. "Even though she is not a Christian, I know Jesus can heal her, so I pray for her at breakfast, lunch, and dinner." Five days later, Mrs. Omir was placed on a ventilator, and the school principal began preparing the fourth graders for the worst. "Jesus, you just *have* to do something," became Ben's prayer. Little Ben's stalwart faith that Jesus could cure his Muslim teacher reminded me of the centurion's in today's Gospel. A Gentile with authority over one hundred soldiers, the centurion knew the power of a distant command and did not want to risk making Jesus ritually impure by entering his house. With most miracles the onlookers are amazed, but in today's Gospel Jesus is "amazed" at the centurion's faith.

Pray

Lord,
I am not worthy that you should enter under my roof, but only say the word and my soul shall be healed.
Amen.

Ponder

What is Jesus's emotional response to my faith in him?

TENTH SUNDAY IN ORDINARY TIME
(LUKE 7:11–17)

Emphatic Compassion

There's more to today's Gospel than simply raising a dead son. In many ways, a mother also has died and is brought back to life. Being a widow and now losing her son, the woman was rendered completely destitute and would have to rely financially on distant relatives and friends. That is precisely the reason why Jesus "was moved with pity for her," the Greek verb *splanchnizomai* connoting a deep, visceral reaction of compassion. This verb is also used when the baby "kicks" in a mother's womb. Jesus's compassion is so deep, arising from the place where life begins, that he touches the coffin—rendering himself ritually impure—and raises the dead. Jesus's emphatic compassion reaches into the very depths of our nitty-gritty lives.

Pray

Jesus,
Your love was not simply expressed in touching actions of love.

You also expressed it in emphatic compassion that rose from the very depths of your being.

Soften our hearts so that we might bring life to the sufferings and tragedies of others.

Amen.

Ponder

What situations move me to an emphatic, compassionate response?

ELEVENTH SUNDAY IN ORDINARY TIME

(LUKE 7:36–8:3)

A Heart's Response to Being Forgiven

Julie came to faith in Jesus as she was serving time in prison and now volunteers weekly in her church's prison ministry to show her gratitude. She's a contemporary example of the women, second-class citizens in Jesus's day, featured in today's Gospel. In the first scene, a woman performs extraordinary acts of gratitude and extravagant love that Simon failed to perform for his guest, Jesus: she washes his feet with her tears and dries them with her hair; she continually kisses his feet; she anoints his feet with oil. The Greek verb *aphiemi*, "forgive," denotes a past action that is ongoing in the present. This woman's grateful, loving response to being forgiven is mirrored in the second scene where women such as Mary Magdalene, "from whom seven demons had gone out," not only accompany Jesus and the Twelve but provide for them from their resources.

Pray

Jesus,
The gifts of your understanding, mercy, and forgiveness are priceless.
May we have grateful hearts that explode in acts of love.
Amen.

Ponder

How do I respond to Jesus's forgiveness of my sins?

TWELFTH SUNDAY IN ORDINARY TIME
(LUKE 9:18–24)

Of Wheelchairs and Crosses

Ed has had multiple sclerosis for twenty years. He has prayed often for healing. "I've asked every saint for help. I've prayed just about every novena. I even visited Lourdes and asked the Blessed Mother to intercede for my healing. Everyone has turned me down." He started hitting the right armrest of his wheelchair and said, "This is the enemy! This is the enemy!" I leaned over, tapped the right armrest, and heard myself say, "Ed, this is not the enemy. This is your path to holiness, and the minute you can accept it is the minute you'll be mentally free from it." Jesus had a unique name for the wheelchair. He called it the "cross." In today's Gospel, he challenges us not to pray it away but to embrace it and then follow him.

Pray

Lord Jesus,
May we follow your example in embracing the cross in our lives, knowing full well that people like Simon of Cyrene will help us in our struggles.
Amen.

Ponder

What is the wheelchair in my life that I refuse to accept?

THIRTEENTH SUNDAY IN ORDINARY TIME
(LUKE 9:51–62)

Three Conditions

Jesus requires the same unswerving determination from his disciples that he had when he "resolutely determined to journey to Jerusalem." He reminds a would-be disciple that personal comfort must give way to the demands of discipleship. Think of Damien of Molokai. To a second inquirer, Jesus states that the proclamation of the kingdom of God supersedes all cultural and familial duties and obligations. This challenged Thérèse of Lisieux's relationship with her sick father. To a third potential disciple, Jesus used an agrarian image to make his point clearly and succinctly: A disciple must be single-minded as he guides his plow forward and not look nostalgically backward to what was left behind. Think of Francis of Assisi.

Pray

Jesus,
You were steadfast in proclaiming the kingdom despite its consequences in your life.

You never ask more of your disciples than you yourself gave.

May your resolve inspire us to
be faithful and unwavering in our discipleship.

Amen.

Ponder

How do I sacrifice comfort, cultural responsibilities, and personal desires for the sake of the kingdom?

FOURTEENTH SUNDAY IN ORDINARY TIME
(LUKE 10:1–12, 17–20)

Sent in Pairs

James's faith was reignited after he made a men's retreat. To promote what he rediscovered on that retreat, James joined a men's group that meets on Saturday mornings. The members of the group hold one another accountable not only for their prayer lives but also for how they are living Christian values in the workplace. "Jesus doesn't want fans. He wants followers who support one another in announcing the kingdom of God," James is fond of saying. In today's Gospel, Jesus chooses seventy-two of his followers and sends them "ahead of him in pairs." The fact that he sends them two by two is a reminder that it can be a challenge and a struggle to live the Christian life alone. We need the support of others as we announce the kingdom in preparation for Jesus's return.

Pray

Lord Jesus,
We cannot live our lives as disciples in isolation.
The proclamation of the kingdom is manifest in how we support one another.
Give us strength when others lean on us.
Amen.

Ponder

Where do I find encouragement in living my Christian life?

Your Enemy Is Your Neighbor

Jesus tells the parable of the Good Samaritan in answer to the question, "Who is my neighbor?" In Hebrew, the word for "neighbor" (*rēa)* and "evil one" or "enemy" (*ra'*) are strikingly similar. Surprisingly, a professed enemy of the Jews, a Samaritan, offers the perfect example of being a neighbor by showing compassion to a Jewish victim. He responds to the victim's wounds, takes him to an inn, and cares for him. And the following day he offers two silver (!) coins for his continuing care—for starters! The parable is unsettling because it reminds us that an enemy has a human heart that is capable of love, care, and compassion. We should be careful how we judge.

Pray

Jesus,

We so easily can judge with the quickness of a stony heart.

Open our eyes and soften our hearts, that we may see goodness in those we label as the enemy or betrayer.

By your loving grace, transform us into a neighbor for our enemy.

Amen.

Ponder

When have I benefited from the love, care, and compassion of an enemy?

SIXTEENTH SUNDAY IN ORDINARY TIME
(LUKE 10:38–42)

Keep the Scale Balanced

The Gospel story of Martha and Mary has traditionally been interpreted as highlighting the perennial tension between action and contemplation. Busy Martha, "anxious and worried about many things," symbolized ministry and action. Listening Mary, whom Jesus said chose "the better part," represented prayer and contemplation. This led to the unfortunate understanding that the religious vocation was superior to the lay or married vocation. In recent years, however, this interpretation has faded as spiritual teachers emphasize the importance of both prayer and action. Action and prayer should support each other. We need a healthy balance of each to be an authentic disciple of Jesus.

Pray

Loving God,
Give us the hands of Martha that are always ready and willing to do acts of charity. Without them, our prayer is shallow and a sham.

Give us the heart of Mary that always listens and ponders your voice in our lives. Without it, our actions can be misguided and superficial.

May we live lives of praise with Martha hands and a Mary heart.

Amen.

Ponder

How do I maintain a balance in my spiritual life?

Tenacious Prayer

After teaching his disciples the words of prayer, Jesus attends to the attitude that must accompany our prayer with the parable of the inconvenienced friend and its explanation. The Greek present imperative verbs suggest "*keep on* asking . . . seeking . . . knocking." Jesus is showing us *how* to pray—with tenacity and persistence, two signs of our absolute trust in God amid our needs. Jesus is not suggesting that every intercession or petition *will be granted*; rather, he is highlighting the fact that a divine response *will be given.* And the response will be generous, because God is sensitive to our persistence and does not act like a miserly, cruel parent. Though our experience might say otherwise because of God's delay or apparent denial of our requests, Jesus challenges us to trust in God's care and concern.

Pray

Jesus,
You taught us how to pray.
May we always remember that our Father is invested in our lives and never ceases to provide daily bread.
Amen.

Ponder

How persistent am I with my prayer requests to God?

EIGHTEENTH SUNDAY IN ORDINARY TIME
(LUKE 12:13–21)

The Monkey Wrench

In today's Gospel, Jesus rebuffs the request of an avaricious brother by reminding him that "one's life does not consist of possessions." He buttresses this teaching with a parable about an obsession with self-preservation. A far cry from wise stewardship, greed rears its ugly head when we think that God cannot be trusted to take care of our needs—and so we horde and hide the essentials of daily living. Death is the monkey wrench thrown in our secret cache and underlines the futile emptiness of greed. Greed's antidote is trust in God and charity toward others—what Jesus refers to in the parable's conclusion as becoming "rich in what matters to God."

Pray

Loving God,
You are the almsgiver who provides for everyone and everything.

Grant us a faith that does not insult you with our worry about daily needs.

Give us generous hearts so that we might spontaneously respond to the outstretched hand, the cry for help, or the person in need.

Amen.

Ponder

What worries of mine insult God?

NINETEENTH SUNDAY IN ORDINARY TIME
(LUKE 12:32–48)

The Mark of a Christian

A popular bumper sticker proclaims, "Jesus is coming! Look busy!" Though the three parables in today's Gospel clearly suggest the sudden and unexpected return of the master, Jesus requires more than the superficial appearance of being busy. He is calling his disciples—and us—to active vigilance since he will return "on an unexpected day and at an unknown hour." "Keep an eye out for Jesus!" would be a better bumper sticker. The fourth-century Saint Basil the Great sums up today's Gospel perfectly: "What is the mark of a Christian? It is to watch daily and hourly and to stand prepared in that state of total responsiveness pleasing to God, knowing that the Lord will come at an hour that [the believer] does not expect."

Pray

Lord Jesus,
We await your Second Coming.

Help us to be alert and prepared with vigilant hearts.

Help us to always do what you ask of us and not grow weary in our waiting.

Come, Lord Jesus!

Amen.

Ponder

In what practical ways do I express my active vigilance for Christ's Second Coming?

TWENTIETH SUNDAY IN ORDINARY TIME
(LUKE 12:49–53)

Playing with Fire

We see a passionate Jesus in today's Gospel who, by his own impatient admission, has come "to set the earth on fire, and how I wish it were already blazing!" Perhaps he is referring to the fire of the Holy Spirit that purifies, separating the dross from the gold. This Spirit-fire will challenge and purify familial and friendly relationships, since all human commitments now become secondary to the allegiance and loyalty demanded by Jesus. This Spirit-fire that purifies is also the very same Spirit-fire that emboldens the disciples to be unflinchingly faithful to the commands of their teacher. A disciple of Jesus must never shrink from playing with fire.

Pray

Jesus,
You came to set the world and our lives on fire.

May the fire of your Spirit purify our hearts from everything that hinders the kingdom from coming.

May the fire of your Spirit, purifying us of all fear, embolden us to do your Father's will.

Amen.

Ponder

How do I know if the fire of the Spirit is burning in my life?

TWENTY-FIRST SUNDAY IN ORDINARY TIME:
(LUKE 13:22–30)

How to Be Spent

When asked if he was saved, Fritz Perls, the German-born psychotherapist who coined the term "Gestalt therapy," famously quipped, "I'm trying to figure out how to be spent." That reply captures an important lesson of today's Gospel. Jesus turns a theoretical question about the number of people saved into an existential challenge: "Strive to enter through the narrow gate, for many, I tell you, will attempt to enter but not be strong enough." One must respond to the invitation to the banquet. We must let go of whatever encumbers us from entering the narrow gate and spending our lives for the kingdom. Great effort and urgency are required, because the door to the banquet will not remain open indefinitely. If we fail to respond and get locked out, our past relationship with Jesus or knowing his teachings will prove futile.

Pray

Jesus,
Grant us the grace and courage to persistently commit to spending our lives for the sake of the kingdom.
Amen.

Ponder

How do I strive to spend my life for the sake of the kingdom?

TWENTY-SECOND SUNDAY IN ORDINARY TIME

(LUKE 14:1, 7–14)

Table Etiquette

Because Luke often portrays Jesus eating and teaching about the kingdom using stories about banquets, a Scripture scholar cleverly titled one of his books *Eating Your Way Through Luke's Gospel.* Today's Gospel is an example. Jesus, at a meal, teaches two lessons about table etiquette. The first is based upon his honor–shame-based culture: never presume you deserve the place of honor at a meal. The same is true for the heavenly banquet: don't presume you are worthy to sit at the place of honor because of your spiritual progress. God chooses where we are to sit. In Jesus's Mediterranean culture, where banquet hosts courted power brokers or repaid an invitation to a meal with a meal,

TWENTY-SECOND SUNDAY IN ORDINARY TIME

Jesus encourages the host to invite those on the margins of society, "the poor, the crippled, the lame, the blind," who are incapable of returning the favor. Such generosity will be repaid "at the resurrection of the righteous." Values are reversed when Jesus is at table.

Pray

Jesus,
Invite us to your table.
Amen.

Ponder

What do my dinner invitations say about me?

TWENTY-THIRD SUNDAY IN ORDINARY TIME

(LUKE 14:25–33)

Radical Discipleship

Ever since I can remember, I've wanted to be a missionary to mainland China. In the early '90s, the Franciscan Order asked for volunteers for the "China Project," the attempt to bring the Franciscan presence back to China. I was filled with excitement and joy . . . until I had a chat with Fr. Myron, a former missionary to China. "Are you capable of learning one of the most difficult languages to read, write, and speak? Can you give up your love for fast food like hamburgers and French fries? How attached are you to your family and friends?" In today's Gospel, Jesus confronts us with the sacrifices and risks of discipleship. He demands not only the total allegiance of our hearts but also of our lives.

TWENTY-THIRD SUNDAY IN ORDINARY TIME

The two parables challenge us to be prepared lest we appear foolish and naïve.

Pray

Jesus,
You require one hundred percent of our commitment.
Grant us the grace never to allow anything to come between you and us.
Amen.

Ponder

How willing am I to hand over my life to Jesus?

TWENTY-FOURTH SUNDAY IN ORDINARY TIME
(LUKE 15:1–32)

Wholeness and Integration

Today's three parables function on two levels. One hundred and ten are symbolic numbers that connote completeness, wholeness, and fullness. In the first parable, a shepherd shockingly leaves his ninety-nine sheep and goes in search of a lost one. As the sheep returns to the fold, the entire fold is now made whole, and the found sheep is reinserted into its relationships. In the second, finding her lost coin, valued at a day's wage, a woman spends more than its worth on buying lamp oil and hosting an exuberant gathering of friends. In the third, the younger son is joyfully and enthusiastically welcomed home. Sadly, the older son feels ignored and is resentful. We are not told if he returns to his familial relationships. These three parables, with the lost object being increasingly more valuable, celebrate not only God's joyful initiative in offering forgiveness but also the spiritual wholeness and psychological integration that divine reconciliation offers.

Pray

Jesus,
May we always celebrate the wholeness
and integration your forgiveness obtains.
Amen.

Ponder

What areas of my life have become lost?

TWENTY-FIFTH SUNDAY IN ORDINARY TIME
(LUKE 16:1–13)

God or Mammon?

In our avaricious society, it is ironic that the phrase "In God We Trust" is printed on our money. That phrase really captures the teaching of today's Gospel parable. Don't think that Jesus is praising the dishonest steward for "acting prudently"; he is not. What he is saying is that "children of light," namely, his followers, should be as clever and industrious in dealing with others as "children of this world." They should not trust in "dishonest wealth" but use material possessions to make friends for themselves, suggesting a life of almsgiving and helping those in need. They will then be welcomed "into eternal dwellings." The word *mammon* is a Greek transliteration of an Aramaic word meaning "what one trusts." Jesus challenges us to live single-hearted lives, not trusting in possessions, power, or prestige, but only in God—as our money proclaims!

Pray

Loving God,
You will never fail us.

Grant us the grace to truly be children of light who only trust in you.

Amen.

Ponder

In whom or what do I really trust?

TWENTY-SIXTH SUNDAY IN ORDINARY TIME
(LUKE 16:19–31)

Sin of Omission

Unique to Luke, today's parable shows us the dangers of being obsessed with wealth. Biblical scholarship offers some interesting insights. The rich man's purple garments suggest extravagant wealth, since purple dye required twelve thousand shells of the tiny murex to produce 1.4 grams of dye; consequently, only royalty and the exorbitantly wealthy could afford it. Our sympathy for Lazarus is heightened since he is the only person in all of Jesus's parables who is mentioned by name. Dogs, considered unclean and undesirable, show more compassion to Lazarus by licking his sores than the rich man. The rich man wouldn't even share his table scraps, typically thrown out for dogs, with Lazarus. His cruel, cold-hearted sin of omission is shocking. The Hebrew Scriptures—"Moses and the prophets"—that called for care for the poor were blatantly ignored by the rich man. Consequently, he ends up in "the netherworld, where he was in torment," while Lazarus reclines in the place of honor with Abraham.

Pray

Jesus,
Soften our hearts with compassionate love.
Amen.

Ponder

Who is the Lazarus lying at my door?

TWENTY-SEVENTH SUNDAY IN ORDINARY TIME

(LUKE 17:5–10)

"A Little Dab Will Do Ya"

There is nothing to get in the spiritual life because we already have it. We simply need to become aware of what we already have, put it to use, and not expect any show of gratitude. Those two sentences sum up today's Gospel. Jesus notes that faith is a verb, not a noun, and, in the words of the Brylcreem hairdressing gel's jingle, "A little dab will do ya." Using Jesus's metaphor, even a person with faith as small as a mustard seed can command a mulberry tree, known to have an extensive and invasive root system, to be uprooted and planted in the sea, and it would obey. The seeming impossibility of such a command highlights the limitless possibilities the gift of faith offers us. And because faith is a gift, we can take no personal credit for any acts that help promote the kingdom of God. Like servants, we are simply responding to the command of our master.

Pray

Father,

May we always put our faith into action.

Amen.

Ponder

When was the last time I put my faith to use?

TWENTY-EIGHTH SUNDAY IN ORDINARY TIME

(LUKE 17:11–19)

Grateful for My Life

In the late '80s, I spent three days replacing the Catholic chaplain in Kalaupapa on the Hawaiian island of Molokai. Once a quarantine site for those with Hansen's disease (leprosy), Kalaupapa continued to be the residence for a few patients who freely chose to live there. One evening, I met Andrew as he left the church. He told me, "Hawaii gives me my housing and a monthly stipend. We are blessed to have a resident chaplain who ministers to us. Every evening, I come to this church to thank God for all he has given me in life. Father, I can't begin to tell you just how lucky I am." Unlike the lepers who "were cleansed" in today's Gospel, Andrew still has his disease but lives in gratitude to a God who has abundantly blessed him.

TWENTY-EIGHTH SUNDAY IN ORDINARY TIME

Pray

Loving God,

We encounter witnesses of gratitude despite the obstacles they endure.

May our hearts be touched by how you tenderly care for us in life.

Amen.

Ponder

How grateful to God am I with all my aches, pains, worries, and concerns?

TWENTY-NINTH SUNDAY IN ORDINARY TIME
(LUKE 18:1–8)

God the Divine Widow

The first sentence of today's Gospel betrays Luke's interpretation of this parable found only in his Gospel: God is loosely likened to a "dishonest judge" whom we need to cajole, pester, and twist his arm. That interpretation calls us to follow the lead of the widow and be persistent in prayer. But there's a second interpretation that is equally valid: *we* are the judge and *God* is the widow. Every day, God comes into our lives and asks us to respond to a situation so that the kingdom qualities of justice, peace, and love can reign. Through people, the situations in which we find ourselves, our deepest feelings, and our most creative thoughts, God fashions a megaphone and asks us to respond. We need to "pray always without becoming weary" to grow in sensitivity to the call of God the divine widow.

Pray

Humble God,
You rely upon us to help build your kingdom.
Help us to keep our ears to the ground and hear your daily invitations.
Amen.

Ponder

How have I experienced the requests of God the divine widow?

THIRTIETH SUNDAY IN ORDINARY TIME
(LUKE 18:9–14)

The Impact of Spiritual Practices

The traditional interpretation of today's parable contrasts the arrogant prayer of the Pharisee with the brutally honest prayer of the tax collector, whose humility wins him divine justification. "[T]he latter went home justified, not the former." A contemporary Jewish biblical scholar offers us a new, intriguing interpretation. It is based on a Jewish belief and the Greek preposition *para*, translated as "rather than" ("not" in the Lectionary). Jewish belief held that just as one's sin impacts the entire community, so too the merits of one righteous person can benefit the community. The Pharisee's fasting and tithing go far beyond what the law prescribes. They have an impact not just on his spiritual life but on the spiritual lives of others, including sinners. *Para* can also be translated as "because of," "alongside." The surprise of this parable is the positive impact of the Pharisee's spiritual practices on the tax collector. "[The] latter went home justified, because of/alongside the former."

Pray

God,
May our prayer and spiritual practices build up the community.
Amen.

Ponder

How have my spiritual practices impacted others?

THIRTY-FIRST SUNDAY OF ORDINARY TIME

(LUKE 19:1–10)

Seeing a Sinner and a Savior

As a young friar in charge of the summer Vacation Bible School, I had been forewarned about fourth-grader Tommy. "He's a troublemaker," I was told. The school principal added, "He's seeking the attention he doesn't get at home." That offered me a possible solution to his cantankerous behavior: I decided to shower him with attention and kindness. Tommy changed overnight. His mother called me at the end of the week and commented, "He told me you noticed him. He's never felt that." A look can be transformative. In today's Gospel, ostracized Zacchaeus, "short in stature" and wealthy by being a "chief tax collector," climbed a sycamore tree "in order to see Jesus." "Jesus looked up" at him and called him down. Being noticed, Zacchaeus suddenly had a moment of conversion and promised to give half of his possessions to the poor and repay anyone he extorted four times over. This Gospel sings of the power of Jesus's glance.

Pray

Jesus,
May we always be attentive to your glance.
Amen.

Ponder

When have I felt noticed by God?

THIRTY-SECOND SUNDAY IN ORDINARY TIME

(LUKE 20:27–38)

Respond, Don't React

It's so easy to mock others' religious beliefs. The Sadducees, who do not believe in the resurrection of the dead, use a wildly concocted example of levirate marriage—which required a widow's brother-in-law to marry her to ensure that the family name would continue—to discredit belief in the resurrection. Notice that Jesus does not reply with sarcasm. Knowing the Sadducees only believe in the Mosaic Torah and not the prophetic writings or the oral tradition, Jesus refers to an important text from Exodus when God revealed the holy name to Moses. The fact that God's self-identity is "the God of Abraham, the God of Isaac, and the God of Jacob" indicates that the three patriarchs continue to live in the divine presence. Jesus trumps the Sadducees' derision with scriptural evidence and proclaims that God is "not God of the dead, but of the living."

Pray

Jesus,
May we follow your example and never reply to someone's derision with scorn and sarcasm.
Amen.

Ponder

When have I openly mocked or scoffed at another person's religious beliefs?

THIRTY-THIRD SUNDAY IN ORDINARY TIME
(LUKE 21:5–19)

Perseverance

Don't get sidetracked with confusion or fear because of what's mentioned in today's Gospel: the stones of the Temple in disarray, false prophets who predict the end of time, wars between nations and insurrections in kingdoms, earthquakes, famines, plagues, awesome sights and mighty signs from the sky, persecution, prison sentences, betrayal by parents and family members and friends, and hatred on account of Jesus's name. As disconcerting and alarming as these are, there is a deep-seated note of optimism rooted in this passage. Jesus will be with us in these turbulent times, offering us wisdom that our "adversaries will be powerless to resist or refute." Divine protection will accompany us amid all our trials and sufferings—so much so that "not a hair on [our] head[s] will be destroyed." Like Christ himself, we Christians remain faithful to our mission, and we trust in Jesus's words, "By your perseverance you will secure your lives."

Pray

Lord Jesus,
Amid our trials and sufferings, grant us the grace to be faithful.
Amen.

Ponder

What situations cause me to fumble in my Christian belief?

OUR LORD JESUS CHRIST,
KING OF THE UNIVERSE
(LUKE 23:35–43)

Remember Me

In today's Gospel, the sneers of the rulers and the soldiers strongly resemble the taunts of the devil when he tempted Jesus in the desert. Jesus does not respond. Luke is the only evangelist who offers us the dialogue between the two criminals crucified alongside Jesus. Like the devil in the desert, the first criminal reviles Jesus and urges him to use his divine power. The second criminal rebukes the first and not only admits his guilt but also confesses that his sentence corresponds to his crimes. And then, as if speaking for believers of all times, he makes the ultimate request, "Jesus, remember me when you come into your kingdom." Jesus mercifully responds, promising the criminal "Paradise"—life with Jesus forever.

Pray

Jesus,
As you hung upon the cross, you continued your ministry of mercy and forgiveness.

Like the second criminal, may we realize our guilt, never hesitate to confess our sinfulness, and always trust in your merciful forgiveness.

Amen.

Ponder

How will I be remembered when I die?

SOLEMNITIES and SPECIAL FEASTS

JANUARY 1
MARY, MOTHER OF GOD
(LUKE 2:16–21)

Mothering the Word

Today's Gospel presents Mary as a contemplative, keeping the words she heard about her son and "reflecting on them in her heart." She is not content, however, simply to pause, ponder, and pray. As today's solemnity reminds us, she had given birth to the Word of God. Saint Francis of Assisi challenges us to do the same. He writes, "We are mothers when we carry Him in our heart and body through a divine love and a pure and sincere conscience and give birth to Him through a holy activity which must shine as an example before others."

JANUARY 1
MARY, MOTHER OF GOD

Pray

Blessed Mother,
We are called to follow your example and give birth to the Word of God by the way we live our lives.

Give us the inspiration and courage to do that among our family, friends, and coworkers.

Holy Mary, Mother of God, pray for us, sinners, now and at the hour of our death.

Amen.

Ponder

How can I become the mother of the Word of God during this new year?

FEBRUARY 22
THE CHAIR OF SAINT PETER THE APOSTLE
(MATTHEW 16:13–19)

Not a Furniture Feast

The meaning of today's feast could easily be misconstrued as a celebration of the sixth-century relic that tradition said had been used by Saint Peter and given to Pope John VIII in 875. But the noun "chair" functions as it does in the expression "committee chair," indicating the person who occupies a specific position. As our Gospel suggests, we celebrate the ministry of Saint Peter who was given by Christ "the keys to the Kingdom of heaven," designating authority to govern the Church. This mandate was confirmed after the resurrection when Christ said to Peter, "Feed my sheep." The power to "bind and loose," as the *Catechism of the Catholic Church* states, "connotes the authority to absolve sins, to pronounce doctrinal judgments, and to make disciplinary decisions in the Church" (553). Through the continuing ministry of the successors to Saint Peter, the Good Shepherd by his gift of the Holy Spirit continues to lead us on the road to salvation.

Pray

Father,
Grant wisdom and inspiration to the pope.
Amen.

Ponder

How does papal teaching influence my life?

MARCH 25
THE ANNUNCIATION
(LUKE 1:26–38)

A Generous Yes

In first-century Judaism, women were considered second-class citizens. They could own no property. In fact, they were considered to *be* property. They were the property of their parents. Once married off, they became the property of their husbands. Women had no possessions. The only thing a woman could conceivably call her own was her reputation. And it is precisely her reputation that God asks Mary to sacrifice in requesting her to become the mother of the Son of God. With a generosity beyond all telling, Mary's response is stunning: "Behold, I am the handmaid of the Lord. May it be done to me according to your word."

MARCH 25
THE ANNUNCIATION

Pray

Blessed Mary,
You stand before us as a model of generosity.

In saying yes to God's request through the angel Gabriel, you show us the dignity that comes in being a servant of the Lord.

May your generous yes be always on our lips as we discern the call of God in our own lives.

Amen.

Ponder

What do I selfishly cling to and refuse to give to God?

APRIL 25
SAINT MARK THE EVANGELIST
(MARK 16:15–20)

An Emotional Jesus

Today we commemorate the anonymous author of the first Gospel, probably written around AD 70. In the second century, the name "Mark" was attached to it, since tradition assigned the authorship to John Mark, in whose mother's house (in Jerusalem) Christians assembled (see Acts 12:12). This Mark was Barnabas's cousin (see Colossians 4:10) and a companion on a missionary journey with Barnabas and Paul (see Acts 12:25; 13:5; 15:36–39). Like the other three Gospel writers, Mark paints a unique portrait of Jesus. Here we discover a Jesus who experiences a wide range of emotions: pity (1:41), anger (3:5), triumph (4:40), sympathy (6:34), surprise and amazement (6:6), love

(10:21), sadness and distress (14:33–34), and indignation (14:48–49). Mark's portrait highlights the human side of the Lord Jesus, "who took his seat at the right hand of God."

Pray

Jesus,
You did not hesitate to embrace our human condition with all its conflicting and contrasting emotions.
May we imitate you in expressing our emotions in appropriate ways.
Amen.

Ponder

What emotions make me uncomfortable? How do I express them?

MAY 31
THE VISITATION OF
THE BLESSED VIRGIN MARY
(LUKE 1:39–56)

Hospitality as a Spiritual Practice

Today's Gospel showcases a unique encounter. Elizabeth is beyond child-bearing years, and yet she is miraculously ready to give birth any day as the baby joyfully kicks in her womb. Mary is young, radiant with stunning faith, and bearing a son. Though the traditional custom of the day would oblige the younger to greet the elder, it is Elizabeth who intuits the sanctity of such a visit by singing of the virgin's role in salvation history: "Most blessed are you among women, and blessed is the fruit of your womb." The Visitation reveals the sacredness of every visit by a relative, friend, neighbor, or foe. Whether planned or unexpected, short or lengthy, each is a divine encounter. Every person is sent forth with a God-given dignity and mission: like Mary, to be a living tabernacle of love; like Elizabeth, to be a welcoming presence to the divine.

Pray

Loving God,
May our presence always be a blessing to those whom we visit.
May we be hospitable to all whom we encounter.
Amen.

Ponder

How hospitable am I to those who visit me?

JUNE 13
SAINT ANTHONY OF PADUA
(LUKE 10:1–9)

Something's Lost That Must Be Found!

Ever wonder why we pray to Saint Anthony of Padua for help in finding lost or stolen things? Tradition says Anthony had a book of psalms that contained his teaching notes for use in the classroom. A young friar who had chosen to leave the Franciscans had taken the psalter with him. This book was hand-copied, and thus an item of high value; a friar, given his vow of poverty, would have found such an item difficult to replace. Anthony prayed the book would be found or returned. The thief was moved not only to return the book but also to return to the Order. The story speaks eloquently of God's investment in the minutiae of our lives.

JUNE 13
SAINT ANTHONY OF PADUA

Pray

Creator of the Universe,
Through the intercession of Saint Anthony, you show your abiding concern for us.

Your loving care pervades and permeates the smallest details of our lives.

May we always remember your personal investment in us.

May we never hesitate to ask for your help.

Amen.

Ponder

How has God revealed divine care and concern for me?

FRIDAY AFTER THE SECOND SUNDAY AFTER PENTECOST
THE MOST SACRED HEART OF JESUS
(LUKE 15:3–7)

What Wondrous Love!

Jesus is often portrayed with one hand pointing to his flaming heart and the other upraised. We could easily misinterpret this feast as a celebration of a part of Jesus's anatomy. It is so much more than that. Today, we celebrate Jesus's invitation to enter his heart and experience a wondrous love that surpasses all our hopes and desires. The fact that we have this feast dedicated to the Sacred Heart is a vivid reminder that most of us just can't wrap our heads around God's unconditional love. We betray it with conditions and try to earn it with our actions. As we respond to Jesus's invitation, let us never forget that God loves us unconditionally—not because we are good but because God is good.

FRIDAY AFTER THE SECOND SUNDAY AFTER PENTECOST
THE MOST SACRED HEART OF JESUS

Pray

Jesus,
Your sacred heart is ablaze with love and affection for us.

It illumines our lives, often darkened by guilty consciences and sinful actions.

May we always respond to the unconditional and limitless love you have for us.

Amen.

Ponder

When have I had glimmers and glimpses of God's unconditional love for me?

JULY 29
SAINTS MARTHA, MARY, AND LAZARUS
(LUKE 10:38–42 OR JOHN 11:19–27)

The Gift of Siblings

In January 2021, Pope Francis ordered the inscription of Saints Martha, Mary, and Lazarus into the General Roman Calendar, to replace the existing celebration of Saint Martha alone. The decree of the Congregation for Divine Worship and the Sacraments stated, "In the household of Bethany, the Lord Jesus experienced the family spirit and friendship of Martha, Mary, and Lazarus, and for this reason the Gospel of John states that he loved them. Martha generously offered him hospitality, Mary listened attentively to his words, and Lazarus promptly emerged from the tomb at the command of the one who humiliated death." As the patron saints of siblings, Martha, Mary, and Lazarus show us different dimensions of holiness: selflessly serving others, listening deeply in prayer, and responding immediately to the divine call.

Pray

Loving God,
Grant us the grace you gave to the three siblings of Bethany.
May our lives be characterized by hospitality, prayer, and an eager response to your call.
Amen.

Ponder

How do my siblings or closest friends call me to a holy life?

AUGUST 6
THE TRANSFIGURATION OF THE LORD
(MATTHEW 17:1–9)

Mystical Moments

Matthew's description of the Transfiguration suggests a mystical moment witnessed by Peter, James, and John. Jesus's face shines like the sun; his clothes become white as light; Moses, representing the Law, and Elijah, representing the prophets, appear and converse with him. There is the shadow cast by a bright cloud with a voice coming from that cloud that proclaims Jesus as the beloved Son. Like many of us in times of intense and gratifying prayer, Peter wants to capture the moment and freeze it. But that is not meant to happen. Mystical moments like the Transfiguration are gifts and graces that God occasionally offers us in order to spiritually invigorate us. They are meant to be pondered—"listen to him"—and, as Jesus charged the disciples not to speak of what happened, they are not necessarily to be shared with others.

Pray

Loving God,
You sometimes grace our prayer with mystical moments similar to the Transfiguration.
May such moments move us to listen more deeply to your Son and follow him more closely.
Amen.

Ponder

When have I experienced intense, gratifying prayer?

AUGUST 11
SAINT CLARE OF ASSISI
(MATTHEW 19:27–29)

What Do You See in the Mirror?

In a letter to Blessed Agnes of Prague, Saint Clare of Assisi referred to the body of Jesus on the cross as a mirror. That's a surprising image. In meditating on the crucifix, Clare not only discovered the blessed poverty, holy humility, and ineffable charity of Jesus, but she also "saw" herself and how she was called to live! In this mystical mirror, Jesus revealed the secret to holiness: live simply, be humble, and above all, love. We do well to follow in those footprints.

AUGUST 11
SAINT CLARE OF ASSISI

Pray

Poor, humble, and loving Jesus,
You are a mirror that reveals to us the secret to happiness and holiness.

You call us to live with the outstretched hands of a beggar.

You challenge us to surrender our ego and die to our pride.

And most of all, you command us to stretch the size of our hearts in love and acceptance of others.

May we come to see ourselves mirrored in your final act of poverty, humility, and love.

Amen.

Ponder

How do I see myself in the crucifix?

AUGUST 15
THE ASSUMPTION OF THE BLESSED VIRGIN MARY
(LUKE 1:39–56)

Gift, Grace, and Blessing

In today's Gospel, Mary sings of God's gift, grace, and blessing. Her being is a gift from God and is awash in grace. She is a vessel of God-given blessings and gratitude. She celebrates divine mercy and compassion that lift up the poor and lowly. She proclaims how God feeds the hungry and has been of help to her ancestors. Mary is acutely attentive to the reality of God's gift, grace, and blessing. At the end of her earthly life, she receives another grace and blessing by being the first to share in her Son's resurrection with the assumption of her body and soul into heaven. The divine gift that Mary enjoyed foreshadows the gift of the resurrection that will be given to us.

AUGUST 15
THE ASSUMPTION OF THE BLESSED VIRGIN MARY

Pray

Blessed Mary,
You were a faithful disciple of your Son.

Your fidelity was acknowledged and blessed by God, who took you, body and soul, to share in eternal life.

May the hope of our own resurrection fuel our daily lives.

Amen.

Ponder

How does hope in the resurrection affect my thoughts, words, and actions?

AUGUST 20
SAINT BERNARD OF CLAIRVAUX
(JOHN 17:20–26)

Pray from the Neck Down

No religious person looms larger in twelfth-century Christianity than the Frenchman Bernard of Clairvaux. He was a man of extraordinary talents and accomplishments that included reforming Benedictine monasticism, preaching the Second Crusade, promoting the Virgin Mary as an able intercessor, and writing on the spiritual and mystical life. His influence on Christian spirituality is evident in the importance he places on bringing emotions to prayer. He challenges us to get out of our heads when we talk to God and pray from the neck down, from our feelings and affections. His emphasis on emotions reminds us that no feeling is unsuitable or inappropriate to express to God.

AUGUST 20
SAINT BERNARD OF CLAIRVAUX

Pray

Loving God,

You gave us Bernard of Clairvaux as a reminder that the human experience includes our feelings and emotions.

They make an excellent topic as we begin our conversation with you.

Give us the grace to follow Bernard's example and never hesitate to pray from the neck down.

Amen.

Ponder

What feelings and emotions do I consider inappropriate to express to God?

SEPTEMBER 14
THE EXALTATION OF THE HOLY CROSS
(JOHN 3:13–17)

The Final Word

While riding his bicycle along the Australian coast, Rob was hit by an automobile that left him a paraplegic. He endured a long road to recovery and acceptance of getting around in a wheelchair. Three years after his accident, I was lucky enough to have a conversation with him. When asked to reflect on the accident, Rob replied, "It's been the greatest grace for me. In my helplessness and dependency on others, God continually reveals his fidelity. God always gets the final word." Today's feast is a stunning reminder of God's fidelity in the face of suffering and death. We esteem, extol, and exalt the cross, not only because it is the source of our salvation but also because it celebrates the powerlessness of death before the grace of God. God has the final word, and as Rob reminds us, that word is always one of faithful love and protection.

Pray

We adore you, O Christ, and we bless you, because by your holy cross you have redeemed the world.

Amen.

Ponder

What have life's crosses taught me?

SEPTEMBER 27
SAINT VINCENT DE PAUL
(MATTHEW 9:35–38)

Choosing the Poor over Prayer

The Daughters of Charity, the religious community founded by Saints Vincent de Paul and Louise de Marillac, wondered if they should continue praying when a poor person showed up at their door during prayer time. Today's saint pragmatically and insightfully replied, "Sisters, since your principal ministry is the service of your neighbor, . . . you are obliged to leave your prayer. Furthermore, if there were no other time to assist him but the time for Mass, you should omit it—and I don't mean only on a working day, but even on a day of obligation—rather than leave him in danger, for assistance to the neighbor has been established by God himself and practiced by Our Lord Jesus Christ, but the obligation of hearing Mass is only of ecclesiastical institution. . . . Still, you must accommodate Martha to Mary and arrange your duties so that both prayer and work may be reconciled."

Pray

Jesus,
Grant me the grace to respond
immediately to those in need.
Amen.

Ponder

When have I chosen prayer over the poor?

OCTOBER 1
SAINT THÉRÈSE OF THE CHILD JESUS
(MATTHEW 18:1–4)

Don't Grow Up

Thérèse of Lisieux yearned to become a saint, but she quickly realized she didn't have the ability to become holy like the spiritual giants of her Carmelite Order, Saints Teresa of Avila and John of the Cross. But God gave her an insight that became the secret to her holiness—and the reason why contemporary believers continue to feel an attraction to her. That insight is captured in today's Gospel and in what Thérèse called the "way of spiritual childhood." She described it as acknowledging our nothingness and expecting everything from our heavenly Father, just as a child expects everything from his or her father. It meant living worry-free. It required always remaining little. It recognized that all practiced virtues are graces from God. It involved never becoming discouraged by our faults, for children fall frequently. Her spiritual maturity is captured in the idea of never growing up.

Pray

Saint Thérèse of Lisieux,
Intercede for us that we might share in your grace of radical dependance upon the Father.
Amen.

Ponder

What childlike qualities do I possess and lack?

OCTOBER 2
THE HOLY GUARDIAN ANGELS
(MATTHEW 18:1–5, 10)

Not Just for Kids

When I was in first grade, Sister Seraphim told my classmates and me that when we sit at our desks, we should scoot over to the left or right edge of our seats and leave a little room at our side for our guardian angel to sit down next to us. Such a memory might make us chuckle and think that today's feast is just for children. But today we celebrate a profound adult belief that has been celebrated down through the ages: God's personal, loving investment in the earthly pilgrimage of each one of us. Through the ministry of guardian angels, who "always look upon the face of [Jesus's] heavenly Father," God offers us wisdom, protection, and guidance. As someone once said, "God has one eye on the entire universe and the other eye riveted on me."

Pray

Angel of God, my guardian dear,
To whom God's love commits me here,
Ever this day, be at my side,
To light, to guard, to rule, and guide.
Amen.

Ponder

How have I experienced angelic protection or guidance in my life?

OCTOBER 4
SAINT FRANCIS OF ASSISI
(MATTHEW 11:25–30)

God Provides

When most people think of Saint Francis, they think of a poor man. And indeed, he was poor. But his poverty was not a self-inflicted denial of material possessions and daily necessities. Rather, his poverty was first and foremost a radical act of trust in God. God was the almsgiver who gave the saint everything he needed. Toward the end of his life, as he looked over his forty-four years, Francis celebrated how God had graced him with his vocation, with brothers, with faith, and with a life of prayer. His poverty was proof positive that God can be trusted to provide abundantly.

OCTOBER 4
SAINT FRANCIS OF ASSISI

Pray

Generous God,

You are the source of everything in our lives—our family, our friends, our clothes, the roof over our heads, and the meal set before us.

In your presence, we can claim nothing as our own, except for our sin.

Give us a radical trust in your divine guidance and care.

May we never insult you with our worries.

Amen.

Ponder

How has God provided for my needs?

NOVEMBER 1
ALL SAINTS
(MATTHEW 5:1–12A)

It Takes All Types

Paul was a persecutor turned proclaimer of Christ. Antony of Egypt lived as a hermit. Martin of Tours was a soldier. Clare of Assisi renounced the wealth of her upbringing. Thomas Aquinas was a scholar. Julia Greeley was a former slave who generously shared what she had with people as poor as herself. Damien de Veuster and Marianne Cope ministered to Hansen's Disease patients in Hawaii. Emil Kapaun was a chaplain in the US Army. Carlo Acutis was a millennial who designed a website exploring Eucharistic miracles around the world. Gianna Beretta Molla was a pediatrician who refused both an abortion and a hysterectomy during a dangerous pregnancy. Today we celebrate the men and women who, each in their own unique way, lived the Beatitudes and are offered to us as role models. No matter our occupation, role, or position, we all are called to holiness.

Pray

Lord Jesus,
You proclaimed the Beatitudes as a blueprint for holiness.
May we live them in our own lives.
Amen.

Ponder

What's my unique path to holiness?

DECEMBER 8
THE IMMACULATE CONCEPTION
(LUKE 1:26–38)

Full of Grace

Ever wonder what it would be like to live in a world without sin? Today's feast and Gospel give us a rare glimpse into that. Both celebrate and commemorate this singular gift given by God to a young virgin. Conceived and born untouched by the effects of sin, holy and without blemish, Mary is proclaimed by the archangel Gabriel as "full of grace." The very moment of her conception sings of the dignity of the human condition as a worthy womb for God. No wonder Saint Francis of Assisi calls Mary God's "Palace, Tabernacle, Dwelling, Robe, Servant, and Mother."

DECEMBER 8
THE IMMACULATE CONCEPTION

Pray

Blessed Mary,

By a rare grace from God, you were preserved from the effects of Adam and Eve's original sin.

And yet, this gift did not take away your freedom. You still freely proclaimed your "yes" to the invitation to become God's palace and tabernacle.

Though we experience the effects of sin in our own lives, may we have the courage to respond to every invitation from God.

Amen.

Ponder

What would my life look like without sin?

DECEMBER 12
OUR LADY OF GUADALUPE
(LUKE 1:26–38 OR 1:39–47)

The Mantle of Divine Love

On December 9, 1531, fifty-seven-year-old Juan Diego met a young pregnant mestiza, a woman of Amerindian and European heritage, dressed in the royal clothes of an Aztec goddess. With Elizabeth, he could have asked, "And how does this happen to me, that the mother of my Lord should come to me?" Though the widower's native land had been conquered recently by Spanish-speaking foreigners, the mestiza spoke to him in his native Nahuatl. That gives us an insight into the answer to Elizabeth's question, Mary's pregnancy, and today's feast: Christ was to be born not only in the Middle East but also in every land and every culture. Indeed, the mantle of God's love covers the entire earth.

DECEMBER 12
OUR LADY OF GUADALUPE

Pray

Our Lady of Guadalupe,
In appearing to Juan Diego and speaking in his native language, you have revealed God's love for every culture on earth.

May your Son's grace expand the size of our hearts so we can love and respect every race, people, and culture.

Amen.

Ponder

What race, people, or culture do I look upon with suspicion?

DECEMBER 26
FEAST OF SAINT STEPHEN,
FIRST MARTYR
(MATTHEW 10:17–22)

Life and Death

Filled stockings hung on the mantel. A lit Christmas tree with wrapped presents beneath it. A battery-powered Santa Claus that says, "Ho, ho, ho! Merry Christmas!" Cookies and milk by the fireplace. The song "Rudolph the Red-Nosed Reindeer." It's so easy to associate the celebration of Christmas with children. Today's feast, however, contrasts starkly with yesterday's feast and reminds us that Christmas calls for an adult commitment. The Gospel reminds us that the splendor of the crib is shrouded with the shadow of the cross. Life and death walk hand in hand in the Christian experience. The birth of Jesus leads to the death of Saint Stephen, and the martyr's death leads to birth into eternal glory.

DECEMBER 26
FEAST OF SAINT STEPHEN,
FIRST MARTYR

Pray

Saint Stephen,
You proclaimed the gospel not only with your words but also with your very life.

May your death instill in us a constant fidelity to our baptismal promises.

May we be inspired to take seriously our commitment to the Babe of Bethlehem.

Amen.

Ponder

What are practical ways that I can live out my adult commitment to the Christ Child?

DECEMBER 27
FEAST OF SAINT JOHN,
APOSTLE AND EVANGELIST
(JOHN 20:1A, 2–8)

The Gift of Friendship

Though biblical scholars doubt that the "other disciple whom Jesus loved" mentioned in today's Gospel is the same person as John the apostle and evangelist, tradition has linked them together as the same person. This disciple's description as being loved by Jesus celebrates a unique friendship and intimacy between the two. At the Last Supper, this disciple reclined in the place of honor, immediately next to Jesus. He followed the arrested Jesus to the courtyard of Annas, the high priest. He is the only male who stood at the foot of the cross. On entering the empty tomb, he "saw and believed." Jesus was blessed to have such a faithful friend.

DECEMBER 27
FEAST OF SAINT JOHN,
APOSTLE AND EVANGELIST

Pray

Saint John, beloved by Jesus,
You are a wonderful example of loyalty in friendship.

You were neither embarrassed to follow Jesus as he was arrested nor afraid to stand beneath the cross.

You were the first to believe in the resurrection of your friend.

May we be given the gift of being such friends to others.

Amen.

Ponder

How do I treat the friends God has given me?

DECEMBER 28
FEAST OF THE HOLY INNOCENTS, MARTYRS
(MATTHEW 2:13–18)

Unrestrained Hungers of the Heart

Today's Gospel portrays a power-hungry Herod who decided to destroy any future competition that could potentially threaten his authority and control of the people. Herod's lust for power is as appalling and tragic as the deaths of the Holy Innocents. This Gospel challenges us to take a hard, honest look at ourselves and ask what are the hungers, cravings, and obsessions for which we are willing to slaughter the reputation, career, or potential of another. It is so easy to victimize others for the sake of our pride, our position in the office, or our craving to bask alone in the prestige or publicity of the moment.

DECEMBER 28
FEAST OF THE HOLY INNOCENTS, MARTYRS

Pray

Jesus,
Your birth as the Prince of Peace threatened Herod and made him respond with violence.

His decision to murder the two-year-old boys in Bethlehem and its vicinity betrays an obsession that has gotten out of control.

May we live with self-awareness and keep our hungers and cravings in check.

Amen.

Ponder

What are the hungers, cravings, and obsessions for which I am willing to slaughter another person's reputation, career, or potential?

ABOUT THE AUTHOR

Ordained a Franciscan priest in 1983, Albert Haase, OFM, is a popular preacher and teacher. A former missionary to mainland China for over eleven years, he is the award-winning author of more than fifteen books on contemporary spirituality and the presenter on five bestselling streaming videos. He currently resides in San Antonio, Texas. His website is www.AlbertOFM.org

---

ABOUT PARACLETE PRESS

Paraclete Press is the publishing arm of the Cape Cod Benedictine community, the Community of Jesus. Presenting a full expression of Christian belief and practice, we reflect the ecumenical charism of the Community and its dedication to sacred music, the fine arts, and the written word.

www.paracletepress.com

You may also be interested in...

www.paracletepress.com